How to Draw Dogs: Step-by-Step Guide

Best Dog Drawing Book for You and Your Kids

BY

ANDY HOPPER

© 2019 Andy Hopper All Rights Reserved

Copyright Notes

The material in question, hereto referred to as The Book, may not be reproduced in any part by any means without the explicit permission of the bearer of the material, hereto known as the Author. Reproduction of The Book includes (but is not limited to) any printed copies, electronic copies, scanned copies or photocopies.

The Book was written as an informational guide and nothing more. The Reader assumes any and all risk when following the suggestions or guidelines found therein. The Author has taken all precautions at ensuring accuracy in The Book but assumes no responsibility if any damage is caused by misinterpretation of the information contained therein.

Table of Contents

Introduction 4

How to draw dog 1 5

How to draw dog 2 21

How to draw dog 3 36

How to draw dog 4 52

How to draw dog 5 67

How to draw dog 6 81

How to draw dog 7 98

About the Author 113

Introduction

Kids have this intense desire to express themselves the ways they know how to. During their formative years, drawing all sorts is on top of their favorite things to do. You ought to encourage as it boosts their creativity and generally advances their cognitive development.

This book is written to give you and your kids the smoothest drawing experience with the different guides and instructions on how to draw different kinds of objects and animals. However, you should note that drawing, like everything worthwhile, requires a great deal of patience and consistency. Be patient with your kids as they wade through the tips and techniques in this book and put them into practice. Now, they will not get everything on the first try, but do not let this deter them. Be by their side at every step of the way and gently encourage them. In no time, they will be perfect little creators, and you, their trainer.

Besides, this is a rewarding activity to do as it presents you the opportunity of hanging out with your kids and connecting with them in ways you never knew was possible. The book contains all the help you need, now sit down with them and help them do this.

That is pretty much all about it - we should start this exciting journey now, shouldn't we?

How to draw dog 1

1. Draw an arc of the head.

2. Add a triangular shape of the ear.

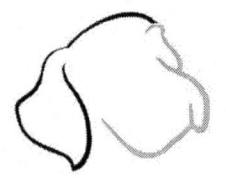

3. Add a rectangular shape of the muzzle and a wavy

line to the right.

4. Add two arcs to the right.

5. Draw one line to the right and two to the left.

10

6. Draw two curved lines of the body.

7. For the paw, we draw an oval shape inside which we draw the arches of the fingers. We repeat the same for the second paw.

8. In a similar way draw the third paw.

add wavy lines on the sides.

9. We draw a back paw. To do this, draw two curved lines and an oval shape. Inside the form, add an arc of fingers.

10. Draw a triangular curved tail shape.

11. For the nose draw a round shape. For the eyes, draw a smaller round shape.

12. Done! Fine. Go to the color.

13. The coat is light yellow, the nose and eyes are brown.

14. Add light and shadow to make it bulky.

15. Color version.

How to draw dog 2

1. Draw two triangular shapes for the ears.

2. Draw two curved arc of the head.

3. On the right, add two interconnected arcs, on the left one.

4. Draw a triangular shape for the tail.

5. Dyeing the pattern on the wool draw a zigzag shape.

At the top of the head, add 2 zigzags, at the bottom, 3.

6. Draw a rectangular shape for the paw.
Below add the arc of the fingers.

7. In the same way we draw the second paw.
Connect it with the body arc.

8. We draw back paws in the same way. On the left, add an arc.

29

9. For the nose draw a round shape. Below we draw the parallel lines of the mouth.

10. For the eyes we draw round shapes and oval around.

31

11. Great! Is done. Go to the color.

12. The color is dark and light gray, the eyes are blue.

13. Add light and shadow to make it bulky.

14. Color version.

How to draw dog 3

1. Draw two triangular shapes for the ears.

2. Draw two pairs of parallel arcs and connect them with an arc above.

3. Draw an oval face shape and an arc of the neck.

4. On the left, draw 3 arcs connected together.

5. Add the curved lines of the body.

6. For paws we draw rectangular shapes and arcs for fingers.

7. On the left, draw a curled tail.

8. On the left, add the arc and in the center the horizontal

line of the body.

9. hind legs draw in the same way.

10. For the nose, draw a round shape and two arches for the mouth.

11. For the eyes we draw two arcs.

12. Done! Fine. Go to the color.

13. The color is light yellow and brown.

14. Add light and shadow to make it bulky.

15. Color version.

How to draw dog 4

1. On the left we draw a triangular shape of the ear,

on the right there is an arc.

2. Add a curved face line and a round eye shape.

3. For the nose, draw a round shape. Over the nose we draw

one arc, under - two.

4. On the left draw a line. On the right we draw the oval shape of the tongue small arches of the teeth.

5. Draw two arcs for the body below.

6. For paws we draw rectangular shapes and arcs for fingers.

7. On the left, draw an oval tail shape.

8. Add an arc for the body.

9. We draw back paws in the same way as the forepaws.

10. For the eye we draw a round shape and a soul for the eyebrow.

11. Done! Fine. Go to the color.

12. Color is white-brown.

13. Add light and shadow to make it bulky.

14. Color version.

How to draw dog 5

1. Draw an oval ear.

2. Add three interconnected arcs on the right.

3. Milking the nose draw a round shape. To the left we draw an oval shape and an arc for the mouth.

4. Draw the vertical lines of the body.

5. For paws, draw rectangular shapes and doy fingers.

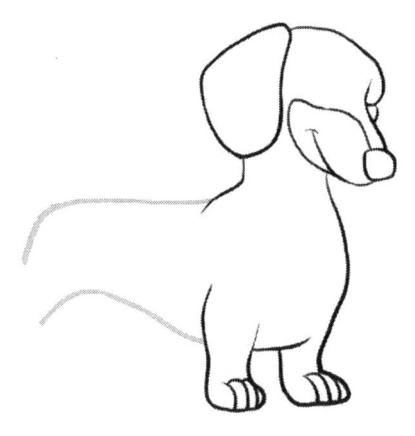

6. Add two horizontal lines of the body.

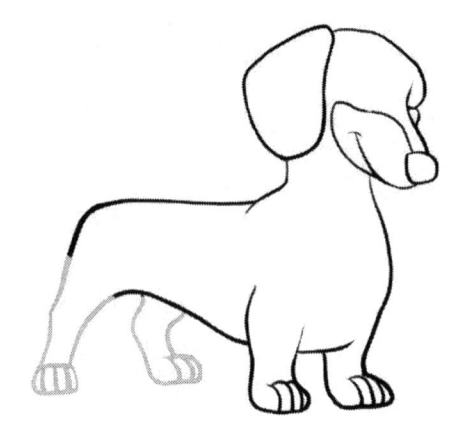

7. We draw back paws in the same way as the forepaws.

8. Add a triangular tail shape.

9. For the eye, draw a round shape and above an oval eyebrow shape.

76

10. Done! Fine. Go to the color.

11. Color is black-brown.

12. Add light and shadow to make it bulky.

13. Color version.

How to draw dog 6

1. Draw two triangular shapes for the ears.

82

2. Draw a curved head shape.

3. For the nose, draw a round shape. Around draw an oval shape and below two arcs.

4. Draw the oval shape of the tongue and small arches of the teeth.

5. On the right we draw three arcs, on the left one.

6. Draw a straight line connected to the oval paw shape.
Add the arc of the fingers.

7. Draw a rectangular shape for the paw and add the arc for the fingers.

8. Draw two arcs for the body.

9. Draw a rectangular shape for the paw and add the arc for the fingers.

10. In the same way draw another paw.

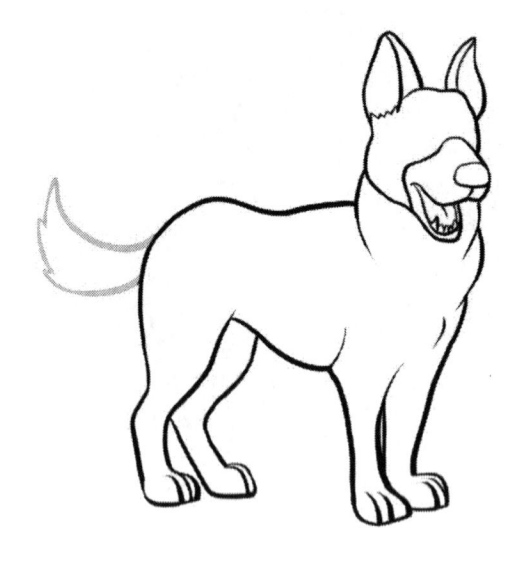

11. Draw three interconnected zigzags for the tail.

12. Draw round eyes.

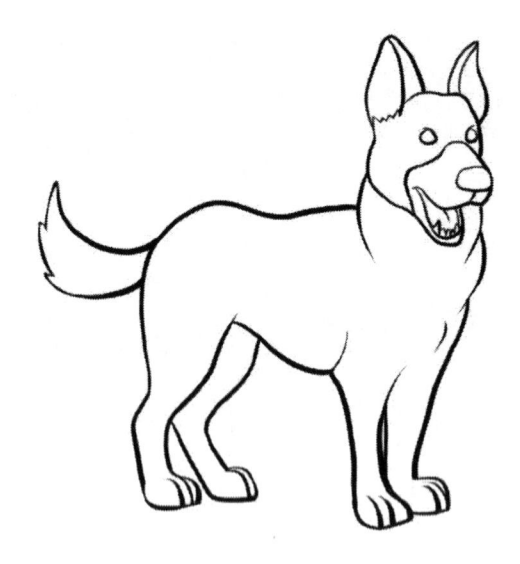

13. Done! Fine. Go to the color.

14. The color is light and dark brown.

15. Add light and shadow to make it bulky.

16. Color version.

How to draw dog 7

1. Draw two oval ear shapes.

2. Draw two arcs interconnected by a third.

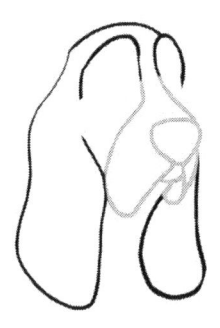

3. We draw a round shape for the nose and an oval shape for the cheeks below.

4. Add the arc for the head.

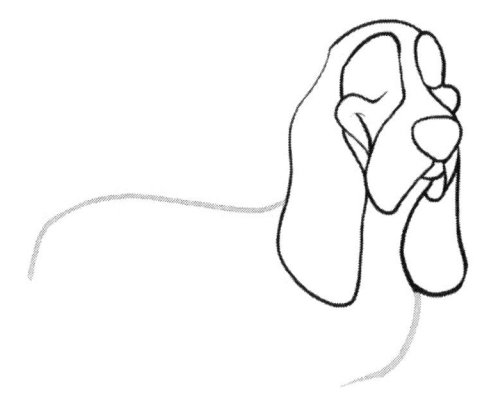

5. Draw curved lines of the body.

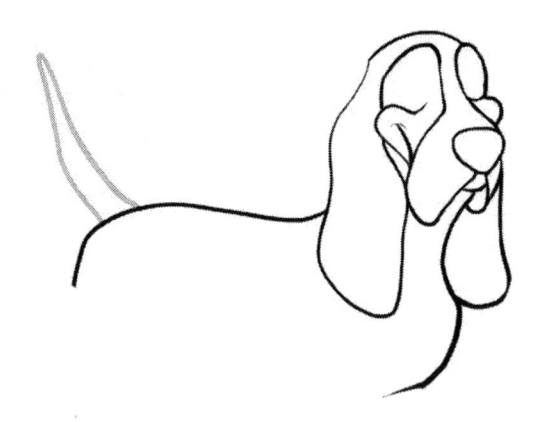

6. Draw a triangular tail shape.

7. Draw a rectangular shape of the paws and the arc for the fingers.

8. In the same way draw another paw.

9. We draw an arc to the body and paw from behind.

10. For the eyes we draw round shapes.

11. Done! Fine. Go to the color.

12. Color is white, brown and orange.

13. Add light and shadow to make it bulky.

14. Color version.

About the Author

Andy Hopper is an American illustrator born in sunny California just a hair's breadth from the beautiful Sierra foothills. After studying Design and Media at UCLA, Andy decided to try his hand at teaching his own unique style of art to novice artists just starting out with their craft.

He has won numerous art awards and has several publications in print and e-book to his credit. His e-books teach the beginner artist how to draw using simple techniques suitable for all ages. While Andy prefers using chalk, pencil and pastels for his own artwork, but has been known to dabble in the world of watercolour from time to time and teach this skill to his students.

Andy Hopper lives just outside of Los Angeles in Santa Monica, California with his wife of 15 years and their three children. His art studio is a welcome respite to the area and he has been known to start impromptu outdoor art sessions with the people in his neighborhood for no charge.

Printed in Great Britain
by Amazon